The Scented Fox

The National Poetry Series

The National Poetry Series was established in 1978 to ensure the publication of five poetry books annually through participating publishers. Publication is funded by the Lannan Foundation; Stephen Graham; Joyce & Seward Johnson Foundation; Glenn Schaeffer; Juliet Lea Hillman Simonds Foundation; Tiny Tiger Foundation; and Charles B. Wright III. This project is also supported in part by an award from the National Endowment for the Arts, which believes that a great nation deserves great art.

2006 Competition Winners

Laynie Browne of Oakland, California, *The Scented Fox*
Chosen by Alice Notley, published by Wave Books

Noah Eli Gordon of Denver, Colorado, *Novel Pictorial Noise*
Chosen by John Ashbery, published by HarperCollins

Laurie Clements Lambeth of Houston, Texas, *Veil and Burn*
Chosen by Maxine Kumin, published by University of Illinois Press

Martha Ronk of Los Angeles, California, *Vertigo*
Chosen by C.D. Wright, published by Coffee House Press

William Stobb of La Crosse, Wisconsin, *Nervous Systems*
Chosen by August Kleinzahler, published by Penguin Books

NATIONAL
ENDOWMENT
FOR THE ARTS

The Scented Fox

Laynie Browne

The National Poetry Series
Selected by Alice Notley

WAVE BOOKS

Seattle   New York

Published by Wave Books

www.wavepoetry.com

Copyright © 2007 by Laynie Browne

Wave Books titles are distributed to the trade by
Consortium Book Sales and Distribution
Phone: 800-283-3572 / SAN 631-760X

Library of Congress Cataloging-in-Publication Data:

Browne, Laynie, 1966-
  The scented fox / Laynie Browne. — 1st ed.
    p. cm. — (The national poetry series)
  ISBN 978-1-933517-26-1 (pbk. : alk. paper)
  I. Title.
  PS3552.R748S28 2007
  811'.54—dc22
  2007012348

The author gratefully acknowledges the editors of the following publications,
where excerpts from this book originally appeared: 3rd bed, 26 Magazine,
Antennae, Aufgabe, Bird Dog, Conundrum, Five Fingers Review, Golden
Handcuffs Review, m. a. g. , Mirage, Titanic Operas, and Untitled.

Cover and interior designed by Jeremy Mickel
Printed in the United States of America

9 8 7 6 5 4 3 2 1

First Edition

for Benjamin & Jacob

Its remoteness from the center of things is what is enduring about a Tale and it doesn't tell the truth about itself; it tells us what it dreams about.

—Barbara Guest

For the spiral-walker there is no plain path, no up and down, no inside or outside. But there are strange returns and recognitions and never a conclusion.

—Fanny Howe

Each word itself is an arrangement
The story must exist in each word or it cannot go on

—Louis Zukofsky

The imund book is the book without an author . . .

—Hélène Cixous

Contents

Book First

THE SCENTED FOX

Letter I.

To a little croft,

rain is known as soft water,
I am using the term "ritual" to refer to the girl of wax. Though human
faces seem not to change while we are looking at them. For example,
the air around a cemetery is said to cause illness. Their typology is
based upon coals of moon.

The dark room had grown waxen. Was there nowhere but here? The
scent surmised a furnace of camellias. Misplaced a storm for a glass
and now that the mimetic body had newly left, I wondered and then
he woke.

Wetted Nomenclature (*a prologue to tails*)

I will now set out to disarrange myself. Comely were thee waters and the flying burrs and this nonsense of a balcony when only she could think of a little shift—the separation and vision of particles. Into the evening which does curl about itself comely as we pair to walk at night, though we walk naught since to watch is naught else but the underside of thought. Grow reticent in asking, this we knew well, to know was asking askew an otherwise wetted nomenclature. So we walk about the furniture and turn astride to ask the wetted frock whose hansom once meted a hem.

I write in whichways aslant and nonne knowest otherwise where from these antiquated words did furrow, it is on no current askew but to pass the harbor lookingly. So lookingly she passed and bemoaning that she had as of yet no contryl of the features of this landscappe she did seek to carve out in words before her. Beholden she was to the myth of blankness, to all forms which had passed beneathe her eyes and to those which had not—but that she had heard tell of through elsewise she knew naught.

Interlude:

My birth shadow is round, a mark of pure silver

A sentence of rime, covered with metlectic mirrors

She goes about as if she were just come out of the mountain

He follows the starling from his perch amid rushes

On their speckled wings he has seen eyes

Mental winds

The Traveling Crystal

i.

Flock to letters

hewy—
frotting

ice, clear, ice crestal

congeal with frost

shyneth in euerie part

in colour waterie

The Forest at Night

She saw a man arrive in a laced hat and coat. They walked side by side during the rest of the evening along the border of an embossed flower, or so it seemed, brushing the fern spores lightly and playing the kazoo. Several town clerks opened their offices along the way and whispered through the Canterbury bells that she must give herself up. Soon they had passed through the embossed town and were approaching the countryside. She was confused when he asked if she would prefer to pass the night in the forest, or to pass through the forest at night, or to pass the forest entirely. Her dress of white silk embroidered in gold had caught along the scenery. Her boots of blue satin appeared muddy. Must the forest be a part of the sentence she asked? Of course it must, he answered, since no one has entered the tale except those who enter everywhere.

She sat for a moment fingering a vine-leaf. It seemed as though she had been dashed from cloud to cloud. Don't cry little cub, he said. To pass the night in the forest, or to pass through the forest at night, or pass the forest as one enters everywhere. And she was to lose herself to what? Though she might pass through herself as the forest is to be entered.

In the morning she was aroused by the lowing of a cow. Apparently the forest had passed the night. In her dreams she recalled a toad pulling her under green water. Washing flagstones upon her hands and knees. She approached the broom growing stiff and dry and no sooner had she clasped it firmly in hand then it blazed in the sense that a sentence may be dangerous. That, though, will depend upon who handles the broom. It did not burn her hands. The border of an embossed flower may bleed, but it will not burn, any more than a girl of wax, who becomes liquid.

She set out in search of a form. Tired of too many dark sepals, and that which emerges single-sightedly.

Letter II.

rain is known as soft water
I am using the word "deft" to refer to a mimetic body. Though ivy faces seem not to chance while we are tangled in them. For example, the vehemence surrounding a furnace is said to cause fault lines. Their typology is based upon the expression about the mouth.

The tiled flowers have grown dim. Was there nowhere but here? The scent surmised a glass full of tremors. Misplaced a hound for a windowpane, a conclusion for a prescription and now that the liminal status has departed, I wondered and he made an explanatory model of his sleep.

Crown of Larks

She saw in the middle of the room face of white, hair of flax, a crown of larks. A person seemed transparent.

She held the red stem of the white rose. The green bud with crème petal edged with spot of crimson. Stem cut, inside the flesh crème sinewy, exuding scent of apple.

To posture the rose is such. As marble marks itself, as a hillside gathers onlookers.

Thus, the rose, more apparent than person.

Only when flushed would she have contained color. Thus, the difficulty of the girl watching was that of an appetite for lifting an illustration of berries from a page. The blood of water is blind in concentration against a hillside transparency.

The Traveling Crystal

The Crystal Letter

ii.

The crystal letter is no letter in hand, no letter of the alphabet, no letter at all.

Alphabed—a place to recite one's letters while in bed.

The letter was that which recommended sleep when once foreshadowed.

The crystal then appeared in the middle of the floor.

The unseen must be accompanied by the seen. It wants to travel, she said, and placed the crystal in my hand.

Does one need to know the history of an object in order to tell?

The object talks.

I, a Little Croft

She has just left off from where she would stare for hours on end and do nothing. I insist she does not. I dare not write this but I have purged my memory since she left.

I do not have occasion to look at you often enough, she said, seated as they had spent several days not out of each other's depths. The days' occasions rose with her, so instead of seeing inside herself she looked outward to loss, and the delicate seasons of this girl upon which her gaze had become caught. Not fastened but held as if she were about to blossom to nothingness, as if the not often enough of her counted occasions did not matter.

She engulfed herself with such silence, such nothingness, which made her subject wish to gather the light she missed, that of her misled eyes, to gather it back and wrap it around her tired shoulders to demonstrate that the inward gaze was also possible, so that there would be no less occasion than memory should suppose. If only to draw on one's name as a shawl, the scent of a white poem, a white peony.

Letter III.

To wood ash,

One can never name the window though I might stand in front of it, as he curls his fingers out toward the light which is also expression. Incantation with no word. So we speak of penetration as towers, a blue building withered in snow. Language earlier than pictures lifts a brow to music.

Gradually tiny centuries. A little thought reflecting nothing, that is to take in a difference. Suppose we are by thought gradually to become, but we can by many partialities fail—a dove represented by maimed glass, entire. So many things replaced by the distance between becomings.

The first hour has named the mortared day we blink. Legs yielded to the pressing landscape. Fingers grasped the first magnificence. Gold interior, of turquoise eye. Still splayed, cold, changed incomprehensibly. Late within and hidden by the circle, the vow.

night, an interlude

where arst thought this spellt upon the hand 'e' of the handemayden gheoste which fathomed blynked and bothered no more.

Thus she begins, werhe soothsayer say little said, little say, sooth, sod or meaning to rewrite perplexity possibly sworn to such the further fathoms of fabric swung so possibly sleep, so possibly supporting the dangers of small fish placed accordingly in our pockets we set out.

and nowhere beginning tapestries
early morning, dedications, a salve
weather maps broken

The relaxing figure draws a windowpane easily with deft blue finger. The glass trembles. Body tangled in ivy. The interrupted moment returns, embeds itself in skin.

Narcissus prism by night

Made darkness white
blunt strokes of paint

A lake in kind
measure swallows
inhabitants

To a reader of lakes:
Fingers flew diametrically
to their onlookers

The forest will pass the night
Why am I kept from it, she asked
stepping out to gather

her senses—
to recant
the glowing narcissus

(the lost scientist, monologue)

He's so flustered he's committing pleonasms
Particularly involving the vessel wall, ordeals of some kind
Full length clone of a novel gene
I live in a room where often
like Rousseau but with no Thérèse, I feed upon bread and cherries
In a library constructed from human umbilical vein.
Come in an hour's time. I shall be there doing differentials screening.
Molecules of distinct schools recline
Upon two armchairs upholstered in horsehair.

end, interlude

Letter IV.

To larks,

Dear audacious journey—A name which has been lost. It was the window through the light, and not the reverse. The white curtain appeared blue ice, roads of their inroads. I write on my lap with the wind locking based upon a fallacy, a region of unsettled land. The light was translucent, confusing January, a spectrum once opaque but now brighter edges prefaced by different eyes slapped smartly. Although pioneering is not often seen.

I find I owe much to the sharpest difference, rasped upon the trail. The following life of the public hill, Mrs. library, rusty manuscripts, powers of the diary we've shuttered aside, countless books, song. Then the trail, snow, carpenters, rudders, and from the letters sleeping in a downpour, waterfowl. The mints in the dish, children falling out of wagons, and the design of making a farm out of personal papers, letters and diaries.

When folly is thrust upon obedience the fabric is brought to bear upon a red background and then the blue window has vanished to chance, the pale sky woven between tree branches, and opposite visions upon a wagon seat as she stared at the endless road. In order to become a schoolteacher she spent most accounts on horseback.

There will be no sleeping late in the 21st century. The tips of the branches are white. And then wouldn't it be better if there were no lanes escorting derision and we simply did proceed to write in a wide archive (I have never met) each dashing jaunt arranged alongside the last interrupted only by softest cheek drawn close in one of the great migrations?

What the roads would bring. If there were—.

Tongue of Woods

They met upon the crimson book.

We have sung, he said, a folded hour. Impossible the way white is sand.

Color prescribes certain entrances both after, and after a reverse.

I must not understand you as you wish, he said, for then we would be of one body. To be of one body we could not meet.

No syllable did not seek reflection in these woods, these double companions

Until all attempts at speech resembled clouds.

Fingers entwined within what they had witnessed

Drenched was the slight lavender gray which suffuses all light, the slightly open buds of magnolia.

The Traveling Crystal

Palimpsest

iii.

Put the rock crystal in the sun and put the warm crystal on your eyes
if they are blurry.

The rock crystal eliminates the malicious fluids of unshed tears.

Its natural art originates from water

Lighten my eyes, pleads the psalmist, lest I sleep

The Book of Slowly

Where does the sentence spirit, he asked, when no longer in search of a question, but formerly to describe a dwelling of such interrogation.

Other universes in smaller dimensions have stronger gravity, said Lady Midtown. It is not forgettable where the spirit does.

What do you mean asked the sentence, tunneling.

How—he says verily this is not my dichotomy, to picture seasons funneling
How—long the leaves tremble viably in hand
How—verily the words gather a bright field of notions
How—waking is further broken if not permitted to slowly

We thank dimensions we are traveling through, she continued. Sentences going my friend, about also when opening paintings.

Describe a dwelling of such interrogation, he said.

We thank dimensions we are traveling through, and this, the sentence contains its onlooker. And there she stood lookingly, to describe the portrait she saw through oval eyes bordered in velvet expression. Her eyes contained the looking premise. They swallowed up to venture what sprawled before, and once below or above or behind her. It didn't matter. Lady Midtown swallowed tightly a contemplation.

Crepuscular she said to the fox. But the fox had deserted her. Nocturnal she said to the squirrel but the squirrel remained diurnal. Ambivalent she said to the gutter, and the gutter remained ambivalent. Where then, she asked, does slowly begin. I am so only a speculation.

How—slowly can you speculate, he asked.

But what does the portrait see, she lookingly confessed.

There is no mid of the town-sentence and not exactly any lady of that, but then speculate, go ahead. The bright field is interior to that. If not forgettable it does not matter how slowly you divine to mend.

for Toni Simon

Letter V.

To a vine leaf,

They said that her mouth was like a rose when she held it in a circle the cold air escaping and whether or not she purposely made a rose with her lips, or held these petals to gesticulate a meaning which could not help emitting fragrance.

Thunder is a rich source of loudness. A sieve considers the shape of a book, the length of an underwritten hand. A hand held in flexion. She searched the apartment, whose parameters in mind were nothing like flowers. Dust flurries. The spiders seem absent leaving only these webs, and working quickly. I did not mean to startle this arrangement.

Matter at base as intelligence, waves, fields, probabilities of roses. The calming influence of sitting was to harbor this necklace of a sentence whose alphabets entwine her lips. Parallel nights upon parallel hips. Hypnotic measures. Circlets.

The Golden Bowl

The worlds in ascending or descending order belong to those who
know them.

That which resides within—a single grace note or inflection before or
after an articulated tone.

Sadness was a dictionary
b for birdsong, blindness
s for seek
d for daughter

A portrait might argue willingness of the daughter-fracture to subsist.
She names as an occupation of surrender, written in a small rising or
falling sign, invisible to all but herself as a stunning flaw, compensated
for by richness of coverings, ample design, willing setting.

To lose one must first possess.

I will put a garland of reasons about your neck
What kind of image has appeared before my eyes
Again and again my eyelids will not shut

Girl of Paper

The girl with red belly

signs cognizant ascent

Where are the letters

without the bronze greeting of winter?

Arbors—

of the seconding green.

The Book of Spinning

Mollie is a girl, an act or spell of revolving or whirling, playing a gramophone.

Her mother, a poor widow, is the act of tossing a coin.

Driven by a coiled spring and not a falling weight, she pastures goats in a birch wood. She hires a motor, she imagines, for quick rowing or sailing.

Mollie had a crook spin.

What a miserable bloody spin, her mother said, a velocity nerve, and gave her a little birch basket, a slice of bread and a spindle. See that you bring the basket home full, she said, to buy seeds, our bioserfdom.

This would require the local rotation of a continuous medium. She wound the flax about her head, as expressed by the curl of sideways loads. She sat down beside a tree (a form of certain angular stationary states) to sing—while the occupation of the goats was to nibble an orbital path through the violets about her feet (their mark upon the skyline).

The midday sun contains the properties of small magnets, she thought, as she ate her meal of witness paper. Then she began, but only briefly, to dance, as the rotation of a body about its own axis, knowing the multiplicity of the tasks that begged her.

Soon she sat down and returned to her clock-studded flax. As a person who spells, especially in a specified way (is a poor speller). Writing or naming the letters of a word. A spelunker.

Once, the spin of her dance seemed to echo a temporal amperage. She looked up and saw what appeared to be the interaction between a crystal lattice and a particle possessing eddies. A maiden in tunneling gauze seemed to be dyeing the atmosphere about her. She set aside her circular-glasses. The forest floors tied the inner frame to the outer one, bracing the entire edifice of the false color image.

Do you spynee, asked the pixie, and before waiting for an answer she took Mollie's basket and laid it aside. Then she began to cast off movements of individual electrons in an easy manner, as if to draw out and twist fibers of light about them as they whirled. They revolved an interlude, subdividing the second, to the songs of grand iconic structures, linnets and siren-thrush.

The apparition vanished. She asked herself as she walked home with her small burden in a careless coil, who was that? If no one asks me, I know. If I want to explain, I cannot. She hid the unspun flax from her mother, planning to make up as soon as fortune would allow, for this miniaturization of time.

The next day when the sun pointed to noon she ate wispy contrails and gathered gigahertz. She then once again forgot her goats and her spinning. At sundown the spectrum was not scarce. The music stopped and the maiden paused. Give me your basket, she said. Look not inside til you are home.

A thousandth of a billionth of a second revealed only birch leaves.

The little goats asked, what ails our shepherdess whose thoughts turn about her as maelstroms?

The tale bemoans its own telling, she answered. Ornate steps propel themselves to the chambers of a cloaked confession. (As she tossed out some of the leaves.)

The sky suddenly green and gray cast an exterior steel lattice all around her in the dusk of whose "now," she wondered. This tiny thread of deceit, a wild cousin, is wound too tightly about my waist. I have been perhaps in a forest imagined which belongs to no one.

Time puddled beside her as she walked, avoiding her destination. The house reached her thoughts, the arc of her neck. Her hair had grown in longer coils along the way. She could have easily mistaken the hills for bedding. Finally she could circle her object no longer.

To her surprise, her mother did not scold her since upon examining the basket, as if to keep a tower from overturning, she found that the birch leaves had turned to _____. Her mother's eyes shone (dark pink areas indicate snow-covered regions) reflecting the future she foretold.

This did not give Mollie much pleasure since once her confession had been made, her mother forbid her to turn once again towards the wood. Now time would become for her an extra skin. She was to stay indoors (reasons for building lofty towers) and to walk as one who carries a full pitcher upon her head.

What has unfastened, her mother asked, now several seasons from her new home, above a spiral stair, revolving in splendid gowns before a many-sided mirror. (An instrument to broadcast her exact whereabouts.)

What is it for you, the mother asked, when dreams appear about you, as many as the leaves in the wood?

Mollie thought, I do not know myself here. What ails the shepherdess whose goats have been divided from her ventures? There is no return to the place of silence from the place of constant fits, from the place of worry to the place of abundance. She did not answer.

The mother continued. What are these thoughts which enclose you?

At this Mollie looked up and spoke.

Thought is that which cannot be parted from matter. My protecting amulet and stirring companion.

And then she was silent, as she turned her fretted bodice in the direction of the wood, where the sun pointed toward noon.

Tooth of Saturn

Emblem sickle

Bewhiskered, wings

Oft an hourglass

Gather newe saltnesse from cloudes

Sope, ashed, hooves, cloth

Letter VI.

To a lost scientist,

Without fault I proceed this nightly intuition. One horsepower is the amount of energy it takes to drag a horse 500 feet in one second. The most conspicuous feature of the whole land is unnatural enterprise. An overblown queen of fortune cards.

A form which becomes what it must in the presence of the actual calamity of time. Talc is found on rocks and on babies. So I sat up in bed avoiding the knock of confirmatory symptoms and had tuned out all signal courtyards as well to avoid description of this state and fit of distant measurements.

Of the strangest bareness imaginable. The dream of a waistcoat agape. The bowl in which I wash my letters is made of brass mirrors belonging to those who lend their reflections. This says nothing of the inscriptions they bear. The mosaic of hours pieced together by the generosity of night falling kindly across anyone's features.

Waxberry, the Forbidden

An apology, for the white berries which must not be eaten, waxberries, for the changing and arrangement of things which no longer fit.

One could only write in the fitting close compartments of a hood. As the mottled attempt of the bird, or lost squirrel who pretends to herself what she has written in a pattern of horse chestnuts has not been.

She needed no longer to go in search of a question. Instead she found herself surrounded, not so pointedly, with one who at that divided into fragmentary wishes.

The wish of the white berries or the wish of the fall, which encompasses like no other form of embellishing garb.

A child is kept inside a map. A cornea of the eye. Concealed vintage chambers.

Darkness were her sleeves a troubled Tuesday tempers. Carrying voices again, inconsolable—otherwise separated drinks of water.

Children are not so small as the paper owls hanging above.

May I come in? (asked the bird). You—may work on your handwriting for a few moments. You are not ready.

The Traveling Crystal

Fragment

iv.

Be it our own hillside, the waxy leaves
I put the crystal letter into my journal
If the crystal put itself there

Owl Queen

In their own homes all women shall be queens. As time passes they shall be once again owls, but keep within a knowledge of divine rite: how their metaphorical children escaped from the ogre and returned to the woodcutter's house with gold crowns upon their heads.

When her grandmother dreams, she holds the child with her dead husband in a delicate wing. She looks through her grandmother's prism to a dream, holding the child who has not yet arrived. The queen can be viewed as her thoughts taking flight. Birth, loss of the other self, the double mirror.

When she had regained her senses she picked up her hand and locked the sentence again, so it appeared to reveal nothing: In their own homes, the birds of Athene were ruled by notational systems found upon bones and horns. Not having these, her sentence becomes a transparent solid body used for dispersing light into a spectrum.

Lucretius, Driven Mad by a Love Philtre

Sewing a hillside into her gown. She took a dried toad and hung it, wound about her waist as a safeguard. Within her booke, she would deliver on the ground, near a stream. Doubts could easily move inside the egg of a goose.

The prince of swords is a glot of wine, returned from the Netherlands to his cursive tower. Shall I tell this to my sister, that his legs are pale like the winter bird's? She came over with a necklace of fern. The river urged her. So direction is jagged to the starling. This she had pieced together between bedstead and woodsmoke, embroidering upon a narrow outline of muslin sky.

She cleaves to a parasol of silence, where no one will watch. A body is drawn to an image: prince, dove, falcon, tower. All fault lines grieve. Image of wax, reshapen. Her hands, embossed, hold the difficulty. The hillside gathers itself. Colors disjuncture.

Broken ash, broken quiver, broken retort, taunt. Let us begin with marrowed speech. Reckoning. First clock of beseeching. Moon as true husband. We are as alike as robins. Fruit bearing ides, in lupercalia. The loss of the person hidden; through hidden acts kalends become new. Mooncloth, a white steel. Casks have been opened by magnetism.

Anemone

The paper bridge escorts us to where we have less estuaries

the front yard trembling

Anemone, he said,

changing the word with the substance of his mouth

Crossing

Beginning nearly upon the same sanctuary which had lulled her. Eight crescents and eight full circles contemplated between the eyes. Each number a color.

At first there was the gold waiting of September

Second the brown and orange fields

Third the dark movement of veils across water, as color descended into the ground.

In December the four corners of the room plummeted until the hearth became their light, and the coldness of the ground promised to guard them.

The fifth crescent was white, as the ice which traced certain hidden flowers in winter blossom. The hazel grove began awakening. As light outlined caverns of clouds whose layers would have otherwise remained invisible. This was when she first sensed movement.

Then red was made to cross the river as she took six steps up clutching a banister of roots, from the interior. Red the color of homecoming. Color of being seen, as a banner, or cape, flame poppies, her dress finally full, describing a circle.

March, the letter auspiciously arrives, as the days of the week return predictably seven, she learns to discern when head is up or down, and small feet press against her.

A tiny green-legged spider clutches eight different directions at once. This is how movement is discerned now from a central point internally.

The baby's head has descended. The green was not green until now. She presses the color onto her skin, which has been present and unseen. The buds remind the cherry trees to blossom, and they blossom from the trunk.

for Elizabeth Lovelace

Letter VII.

To a waxberry,

Lime is a green-tasting rock. Robin's egg and bat skeleton. He crawls down the ramp at a rapid pace, reaching to touch the false water, covered in a layer of dust. The days in their sequential ceremony repeat themselves and I take care to bury them deeply, so that no animals or persons may come across them. This is said nonchalantly. A big "a" as he opens his mouth and gathers the bread. The gesture undone and repeated a thousand times. This is my memory of the liminal status of false dust. A tiny array of picture-settings of dusk, all lined up along a window's edge, tangible tree branches in bud.

I search the dross of mechanics and otherwise fabled advice by placing them in a fast flowing stream and may borrow that sense of purported substance by traveling thousands of miles in a morning and yet we have not as yet left the house. This mode of locomotion compared with the memory of March—ascended a pitch of elevation where we walked single-hipped, the other occupied by a child who seemed no longer a baby though with baby skin and baby cheeks. Ascended polarizing white light at an angle impossible in practice.

The Traveling Crystal

Sought

v.

There you stood at the top of the stairs, the found sentence or the found bedroom. Where had she placed the traveling crystal?

Dressed like a portrait, there you stood at the top of ordeals of every kind. I kept opening the page to 'morning and evening star,' and the refrain kept repeating, *unnecessary noise harms the countryside.*

Birds, succumbed

Work upon that statuary has kept her busy. Something new at times must be forbidden simply to allow abandoned thoughts to prosper. They must be rescued. Nevermind that she wears a necklace of nuts and burrs and a bracelet of beans. So to assume that one must always expect the new to emerge is expecting a caller to call and to never be at home. Nevermind her robe of coarse cloth, her headdress—a pullet feather. To be present then one must rearrange the furniture which cannot be seen.

She goes about arranging. This displacement is thus an hour which despises no time. The old is everything spoken through. To deny that is to deny her existence. New thought is new, very becoming, as if—she imagines straightening her plastic gloves—she might hide beneathe the faux pearl button which completes her wrist. She has been warned against backward thought, but she stands in coarse shoes of felt and replies to the visitor busy reinventing her interior that to avoid backbending is to deny that the construct of time is not hidden from those hands which turn away from the cascading hill. There is no elsewhere without this present which occurs simultaneously.

Next she must find some kindling. This is always the problem proper. She works quietly despite the sound of thought rushing. Light is permitting, though she anticipates interruption, another difficulty in being home to one's self. Broken objects she shall not catalog here. Certainly she sees the challenge of buildings standing only to sway and subvert the eye but that doesn't make them brilliant. And what of an afternoon, as an increment which may be useful, asks her visitor. She drops her bouquet of chicken feathers upon a worn satchel, rearranges her blue yarn stockings and then sits beside the bouquet on the satchel, as there are no other objects in the room. She considers that the birds outside her window have succumbed to composition. There is something in the interior of thought as she passes through days uncertain, but certain that to consider an afternoon an increment is no way to rescue the possibility of residing firmly within it.

Must we divide? They are strung together, she replies, fingering her bracelet of beans.

for Juliette Aristedes

The Stone Boy

The boy and his pine

plume trimmed

without ruins

He cries

altogether   paper

The Perfumed Pear

How might starlight be constructed?

She held the difference between what she knew and what could be
shown.

Early he got up, went to the riverbank and filled his pockets with
small white pebbles.

One syllable, a stone of this, he knew.

She spoke as if the night had not a choice but to side with her.

To make a star exactly, she said, one needs only indelible light.

He looked about the white and gold premises. The movements of the
bat resemble those of the swallow, he said

Earlier that day they had walked along estuaries searching for the
neck of the white egret

as if they had been living the lives of the shorebirds

The dropping buds did form a circlet of white sky pierced by thicker
branches.

She continued hanging linens to dry by the fire of rosemary and
almond shells.

Then went out to feed her roses.

She saw the upward cascade of the pear tree

Assuredly, one need not bind the color to find it rests upon these very lips

A gown lit, consumed by blossoming stars

Dybbuk

It is writ, the harbinger. The lune's attractions. I go on foot. Seraphim in plural. That is my custom. Arched relevant digits. Giddy horses. Down the calm flower's vapors. I am a coachman not afraid of wind or snow. Thirsty for mourning violas. My ablutions, my spells, my fasting like blank sand glots glisten with blue corollas.

A girl is sitting with her face to the wall. Journey beyond baseness. Her song amiable as a martyr rises. You are yielding empty pails. She is serving sacraments of perfume to the tired. Souls returned as fish and plants.

A bride must not be left alone in a cemetery.

Her father stands without regret, deliberately lost. The dust, you shall dance. He repeats, You shall dance the dust of the poor.

The crustacean of the river has a coiled heart. Soon also you will weep. Take this cane and knock upon the grave. There, paved with ribs. A worm can enter a fruit, jade summers and jewelbox gates. Let seven horns be brought. Let her wear a white shroud.

The Book of Atrocities

So and so died from 1750 to the present. He expired in 1750 and later died. She died in 1750 and is still dead today. His mother died in infancy but lived to build the log cabin in which he was later to reside.

The Prince's Wood Ash

To beseech whose powers, a prince laying aside his crown often forgets his parameters. When out within language, the wax rose requires one to draw in the house at its banks. To seek not an object but a process, the object sways desire to practice. The prince objects not to the house, nor the rose, but to the illusion which banishes the countryside. He believes it impossible to object to the countryside. This is his internalized speech, so he supposes walking for walking's sake is not to be considered aimless. A container for thought is merely a diameter. A borrowed swan. He may cut and paste hemispheres and bottle the wood ash for approaching occasions. But never to step away without it, he draws the rose to circumnavigate the house.

Letter VIII.

To night,

She wanted to write with her hand foretelling the edge of something not yet named. Not the physicality of the clover wild when you wade through it, up to your chest, the floor upon which she sits or otherwise less restrained to speak in sentences which were meadows opposed to pasture, not lined in parallel ridges, or round enclosures, or even the thought of perimeter in order to calculate the exact area in which one stands in relation to a guidebook promise. The motion made us all accustomed. It was of no matter since the physical world surrounded her physicality, which surrounded something more essential than a body reclining upon uneven floorboards. Then this telling or "falling" allows her an undefined space in which there might be no omissions, no categories, no careful constraints.

Interlude:

I dress
my vowels
oddly
Peaks covered
with garments
of birch

Simplicity is
an even
fitting,
a diagram of snow
to define white.

Naught trembling
linen maiden

No pleated coif
inherited
but one
deliberately
unbound.

Shall I
separate
even now
gold
from circlet

interior from
chamber?

Speech requires
an opaque
mistress
whose steps
appear mineral.
A winter song closeted
by staves.

An Insincere Tale

1

She must take her hair down before she begins. Ten o'clock. The night contains no nightness. The black could be ostrich feathers. The backs of penguins. A pincushion for piercing thought. She belongs to her tale in the same manner in which her tale belongs to her. But her tale contains no element which compels her to follow it, so that even though it was her place of residence, she did not believe the tale she found herself standing within blankly while the dark sheets of tepid night fell around her soundlessly. If she closed her eyes she might always remain somewhere unnameable, and escape the story in which she must participate. Must I participate, she asked. One certainly may decline. Or, do those parallel forces like parallel nights finally propose an invisible leverage which brings even the recalcitrant to dance?

So she stood within her paragraph, upon a little lined shelf, sheets with dark letters crashing around her head. Thunder, she thought, but they used to flutter like bouquets. And she wished to bury herself in the fragrance they once foretold.

2

She must gather posies plied before she begins down the narrow pathway. Ten o'clock hedges gleam in summer bright. Night contains no darkness this far north. The light quakes beneathe her tread. She belongs to her wheat-field in the same manner that her fingers have been tinged. But her delight contains nothing of the heron and the lake. So that even though it was her sanctuary, she did not believe the tale she found herself eyeing at the rich day-close while little twigs broke about her. If she closes her eyes she might always remain somewhere unnameable. May I intuit the narrow pathway through the old molehills, she asks. One certainly may interrupt. Or do those meanest gifts where'ere we find them journey with nimble feet from one milking to the next?

She stood within her bramble, upon a knoll oddling, while the thorns whistled around her mealy gray. Like slate, she thought, but they used to drone as the bees. And she wished to refashion her neglected pastures to match the prismatic hives of comb.

3

She must take in the first critic to anoint sinks before she begins to pontificate. Ten o'clock is masked by the soft light hidden by the green shade upon her desk. The darkness could be a platitude which opposes the natural features of the landscape but she would not consider this opaqueness. She sits between objects properly placed, figures well grouped.

She belongs to her index in the same manner in which her preponderance belongs to her setting. But her sincerity contains no element which compels her to claim it, so that even though it was her epistemological problem she did not believe the objectification she found herself within, prompted while rhetoric echoed about her to a powerful degree. If she closed her eyes she might always remain somewhere unnameable, and revivify the suggestion for which she had become elaborately equipped. Must I imply absolutes, she asked. One certainly may defer to states, assertions. Or, do those graceless errors like unfortunate solemnities proffer the only components accepted as recognizable notations?

So she sits upon her dovecote, upon an occasional drawing, imagining lines of perfect rest surrounding her head. Clouds, she thought, but they used to be fingers. And she wished for those hands to grasp her head firmly, and guide her towards making the mind more temperate.

for Lisa Robertson

The Traveling Crystal

Letter

vi.

(If the crystal put itself there—in the middle of the floor, and didn't fall off of a shelf, or out of your hands—it's quite amazing. Crystals are known for their ability to travel on their own. As for the meaning, I think it wants to travel with you. In any case I believe that it is definitely meant for you to keep. It is communicating with you in its own language and cannot be exactly translated.)

Sentencing

There is more waiting than one thought possible, began the female sentence. But how then must one proceed?

Simply, replied the pear. One proceeds. One need not wait.

Not wait, asked the sentence?

All will befall, replied the pear, and none will be forsaken. One may lose regardless of gazing lookingly. This episode of yours is hardly less meek. It will befall everyone.

But when the sentence gazed into the pear and saw herself reflected in its golden skin, she knew otherwise. How then can my befallen state be the same as any other?

When one has just heard brave news, replied the pear, that one has been granted a wish, the sentence must contrive to complete itself.

Confound the one who first distinguished the hours, continued the sentence. Thus, my body becomes a question.

Who assembled the first sundial whose shadows plague these letters to no end?

The Tower

The flower is always within the almond.

The tower is perfectly round, of dark stone, containing only light from a narrow window.

The girl within dreams she is the bud, hidden by a profusion of blades.

Constantina, still enclosed, tightly folded seed.

Is the tower the seed which encloses, or is this seed the sitting room of mind?

She was brought to the tower unwillingly.

To follow a color not in the spectrum, a lure.

For there to be color, she was told, while stringing a scarab onto an amulet which she now wears about her neck, something must be absorbed.

One color is the absence of all others.

At that moment, all of her possible habitations vanished from sight.

One absence is the lover who displaces the spectrum.

She feigns sleep like a curl and dreams of her past life where things had once to be accomplished.

Interlude:

Green gravel

washed

in milk

and otherwise

what matter?

She will lie

down

her every

thought

to lift

the lavishly

loved.

To be written

in thick sheaves

inscribed

upon loaves.

Ceremony for A Man Possessed by the Spirit of a Lion

He writes a letter, but he has not sent it anywhere. A lion possesses no envelope, no postal intent.

His wyfe complains, "His mane is so dense and bright a tangle that I cannot see beyond. When he wraps his arms around me in sleep I feel I can hardly breathe." In the daylight she mails the letter to the village elder and receives the following reply:

To the Wyfe of the Lion,

Youth must become warrior
Boys decorate their faces and dress their grandfathers with warmed wine
A competition of charms ensues

combine:

ebony
gold flake
sibylline vow
reef-star
nest of sepia mouse

———————

The lion attempts some verse for the competition of charms:

The sky too devoid of color and not thickly white as I require on winter days,
no tint then, hollow-cheeked with pointy barbs of trees prickling through
and too much somewhat yellow in my eyes among the buildings.

He flings the paper aside and says obligingly to his wyfe, "Let us take
a drive in the country."

She however is busy peeling a sibylline vow from the dead leaves
surrounding a green stem. Though dried and darkened, the vows
appear as adornments. "To simply put things down, she replied, "I
cannot."

What is the law of change he asks.
Night darkens, she replies.

———————

The elder officiates as the ceremony begins: Sea lilies, inhabitants of
the deep, have a cup-like body, beautifully transparent skin. Yet this is
abhorrent to the mud eel. Arrange the plumage of white trees to greet
any setting and stillness mounts the eyes.

On the occasion to be returned to being a man he must walk into the
aqueous center. At the request of a very near memory, he returns to the
occasion of glass and preliminary rolling.

———————

The lion drinks the potion. He moves stabblingly across the stage. Branches blackly confusing the landscape, leaping straight up or veering about, scrawl his steps.

The body being that which is most visibly seen, his wyfe's words are blotted out by her motions.

When he awakens, writers liken him to a peacock upon a lapis lazuli mountain.

I promise you this, he speaks, raising his head, no more than a sentence in a book, written for what has been lost.

The Traveling Crystal

Oblation

vii.

Place the crystal in a vessel of water at new moon

Steep overnight

Gather infusion at dawn

Mix with dew from lady's mantle

Carry and offer this potion to a sparrow

The Book of Miss Fortune's Tavern

Or, knotted plove nest at candlemass. An inkling of figs. A maiden ascends. One may not sleep within an onslaught, the monarch or the butterfly replied, a treble molten. Bridled, landlocked.

Method of physick, 1652. Roof stork thawed loess. And if she be unskilled of pains of travell admonish her to hold and stop her breath strongly. Thronged barb birch, fossiliferous. And let her thrust out her flanks with all exasperation. Traceless prattle moss dredged. Stone plaited. A tale of February quickening.

Her feet are fan-shaped, skin becoming transparent. Drenched porcelain. Coral fleet. Deny she could not, clear light approaching. Fowl wreath evoked prow. Cold, as winter prose is seldom no bird. Her eyelids will meet and temporarily fuse. Before she disappears entirely— thieves coo.

She shields her eyes. Peat migrants brood lettered. Nameless fir. She shields her breasts from what lies beneathe. Ivory plinth. Quill geese felling noon. The day is crimson. Plowed folly. She carries vacant lots upon her back. A bird's thought knawing. She carries percentages which plague the nights. Hunt woven, threshed. She carries one child in her arms and one beneathe (her dress). The older child mirrors his own need for privacy. Are you hiding, he asks? Brightness of expression blemishes hands with light. Doorstone hedge doves.

Her steps are upon moss, stone conditioned by mud, toads of winter. She carries a candle, beside the paper cows and horses, betwixt inner drawing rooms, beneathe closed doors.

The mind, she conjectures: A cypress shawl. Veins of the iris. Gesture of figure. Abandon and inhabitation of the body. Sky furrowed away.

To find a form of ascent she does not dismiss: the menaced, the latched, strung dregs, an echo returned to a bat's ear, the management of a long gown, nesting seabirds.

She carries black bile in a philtre, commits poppy encryption, serves warmed wine in a competition of charms. Performs bloodletting.

She cleaves to granite bounds, steps which cresses impale.

Locates this carnelian sheaf which rests upon winter. Ivy oxen. Spindle sowers. Twisted wisteria. Windflaws.

An oath which combs the hedges of her approach.

for Stacy Doris

Constantina

Eventually flower petals must be collected. The floors must be cleaned for children to crawl upon. The surroundings are brimming. The tower is lost to mail, lists, dust, and long-legged spiders. Conversation and thought beyond the tower interrupt the bodies of the lovers who search for the spectrum beneathe the scarab, the breath which holds the hours intact so one may see one's perimeters.

She retreats to her little dovecote. She looks about to find herself within no tower.

Milk Perhaps Does Not Suffice

We listened to their approach, with whom were they to lodge? The cherry petals, to where are they hurrying. White sky bright against white curtains. Orchids are thirsty so fill with pebbles the white blossoms. A crow walking down the path of morning writes upon a plain white field.

The life of a young maple leaf: dear mommy, here is a book I picked out for you. Sidney the Fisherman. On the cover is a cupid playing darts, another on the other side of a woman embossed, holding a scalloped fan.

The day was so rain-y, *cinnamon buff or cinnamon drab*, that Car-rie and Ber-tha had been forced to stay in all morn-ing. But in the af-ter-noon, *skull relatively long and narrow*, the clouds broke a-way so bright-ly, *very pale form (lutescens)*, that down went dolls, books, and work and off went the chil-dren for a romp in the fields (*Rather small, richly colored forms*). They talk with a drawl, without purpose, without paragraph, without considering. As they were pass-ing through the front door, the great depth of the inner re-entrant triangles.

To be generous at times requires a lapse of paragraphic intent. With a drawl continues the ink.

I cannot bear to be apart from my si-lence, said the young lad-y. What does one do in the country? To approach various views. But then to inhabit a vista, to imbue wafting color. To finger the scent of beach agate, examine hands of sand. Elixir driftwood. Tooth dried bulb of seaweed. To crawl towards or away from what no longer seems cold, but merely motion. Or to approach sound the color of which from a distance is blue, but then white, bubbly.

Imbue the hidden truffle. Creature saved from a shipwreck. There are wrecks that are not adventures. Does she love an-y-one?

A young la-dy play-ing and Mr. Von Horn sing-ing convex, *broadly oval in out-line and completely adnate.* The bridegroom arrives on a white horse. Ten or eleven sunrises in the five days she was there.

It is judged that this modification follows choice of habitat. I am ver-y mis-er-a-ble said Wil-lie (*distinctly yellowish face*). There is no-body to at-tend me. Twenty miles of north-northwest. Low cov-er.

Mam-ma has gone out (*this ancestor is arboreal or terrestrial*) and she told nurse to 'muse me' and she said it was too damp and I could 'muse myself' by sitting here, and it does-n't muse me at all. *Pro-tec-tion for the rem-nant.*

Ber-tha sud-den-ly look-ing up saw that it was grow-ing pret-ty dark un-der the trees. *Win-ter pelage unknown. Upper parts a trifle paler than chaetura-drab. Distinctly flecked and grizzled.*

And that the place in which they were did not look fa-mil-iar. *Time of molt-ing.*

The granular or pours appearance of the frontal. Well said Her-bert to punish you for run-ning away (*soft sediment habits*) I am go-ing to get down and make you all ride home on Rob's back.

While the lit-tle girls were mount-ing they shout-ed with de-light.

The Traveling Crystal

Booke

viii.

Three times she stood up, ran out with the booke

fell to sleep with the booke on her face

Cristalla slept beside her, continuing her reading.

Her hand approached the object

(birds that from the brink of liquid chrosta sip)

she dared not to touch

Cristall of the pearle-bright booke

The Girl of Wax

The girl of wax is plausible. An unfixed entity. She frequents the rose coast to pluck plasticity. What is real fastens pretend. What is pretend—the furthermore real. She is liquid, solid, necessity.

She has spilled her premonition upon volumes. Perhaps the counter desired to be bathed in tea. There is a formless experience. Where she spilled tea on whoever was king. In that history, if the tea hadn't spilled he wouldn't have been king.

Then she goes outside to tell that storm to be quiet.

Hair flew in rivers and rivulets of coal
in pale fronds her fingers flock to the child's laughter

She believes she has lost the pretend coast where once she had gathered an estuary, though one cannot misplace a pretend landscape, though the description might be awake elsewhere, borrowed. This is not seen, only a flutter and the dark rivulet fallen across one's eyes. Wax flowers alongside, these have been riveted to a cloth. Burrs as well and brambles held in place by fasteners. The view, more or less, is the painted imagined. One edge of color is enough to lead eyes astray. True light is the only member which must ring false and fall upon the palm of an ashen hand.

But also she wanted to speak of the unspeakable. He has torn one of the owl's wings. That which gathers and falls along the pretend coast. It is not as shocking as the wet smear of madrona bark, smartingly red. One may gather there only news which has no surrounding. The owl with one wing continues to wait. Surrounding itself with unspeakable vistas. She wanted to speak of what she dare not speak of. The body in part a gesture, surrounding a jet black night. A superstition, that the days followed the nights and so forth. The night, a gladdening gesture. One's own thoughts—if we cease to see them passing—approach non-seeing acres and rejoice. Thus to say one has lost the pretend coast might be to presume that one is finished with artificiality. One is finished taping the torn wing. Therefore complete. But, she may say, she is intrigued by the beauty of falseness, here where all tasks have completed themselves.

The Traveling Crystal

Historie

ix.

Crystals of alum

Silver tartar

Venus copper sugar

Reduced to salt by sharp points spirite of nitre

Crystals of Mars

Crystal detector

Crystal diode

Rectifier, receiver

All kings vnder the clowdys cristall

Crystal sense

Crystal lattice

Crystal violet

Crystal-dropping eyes

Understory

Each step we advanced, the seagull would take several away, but did not fly off onto the water for about twenty minutes, at which point the baby held up his hands and said "abvvba." The seagull is neither his brother, twin, or actual double. This is not the story which leads like a finely turned road up to the entering of a carriage. Nor is the bird to be so inseparably connected with him that its treatment or fate will shape his aspirations. Nor is this any story at all, by the limits of the conversing of the chestnut mare with the bay. Because the stones define a portion of reality does not suggest they function as releasing mechanisms. Nor is there a stone mansion, or a finely turned road. Nor will the bird impart aid to a child who is too thin or has difficulty breathing. Hair glistens but is torn and caught by little hands. A blue scarf slips from a winter neck and catches along puddles of mud in the wheels of the stroller.

Burn the scarf and keep the ashes to be used as a drink by mixing with water. This is the advance of the next chapter in which he fell in love with the seagull. Nor will objects buried with the ashes influence the course of the infant's life. She has been enamored with the story which approaches the stone cottage, the routinely turned winter road, with all of its letters carefully carted along pink and gray stones. Inside the coconut dipper (which has been lined with ashes) is a piece of paper on which something has been written. But there are no longer any stones at all along the dirt or concrete or asphalt or faulty wooden floors. The dipper is covered and buried under the house where it remains for two months. But there have been embedded many novels—though she wears none of these, no stone cottages about her bare shoulders. Instead a footplow, a shover pick. A spindle, loom, hoe, rubber bands for weaving. No winter roads traverse, as yet.

Considered too valuable to be moved from place to place during ceremonies, this bundle buried under the house is represented by a drawing. She often reread the tale which approaches some vestige of a home, drawn as a bilobed organ with a cord depicted in correct proportion. In the original drawings the object is colored dark red.

Book Second

Tales In Miniature

1

furrow
tigrish
till

2

woodcutters
pebble
prattle

3

cave
dress
rogues

4

mill
leaf
dross

5

cat
periwinkle
tine

6

trapping
window
bleat

7

banister
water
wait

8

messenger
harp
rime

9

maiden
test
repetition

10

pard
cleft
ash

11

letter
falcon
hidden

12

rue
daunt
twine

13

stallion
broken
ribbon

14

wintry
purse
dew

15

braid
cliff
axe

16

oarsman
leaf
queen

17

purpled
snarl
lilt

18

wince
sap
cloak

The Traveling Crystal

Found

x.

Prehistorically they traveled by torchlight, twelve miles into the cave. With simple instruments they mined the cave walls for crystals which they used to build simple chrystal'd streams, to mend solitude, for scrying, as balm, and often to carry teares in which they were able to view the sorrows of others.

Book Third

FESTOON DICTIONARY

checkered: careful in the observance of quickfire and ceremony

nightlatch: funnel-shaped flowers of various colors

rareripe: nymphs guarding the golden apples of Hesperides

superstition: the spine of a herring with ribs extended

braid: to interweave an ornamental alexandrine about the wrist

pettifog: a tendency to soften butter

ketch: to shackle the feet of a horse at pasture, entangle

lambrequin: between larval and adult forms

quiddity: in crystallography, a form in which the faces intersect

purr: a girl doll, puppet

fetlock: to adorn or edge with metallic tread

hoof: the quality of being strident. We struck the main road impetuously.

transfluent: to utter such a sound

labellum: to move in ripples or with murmuring sound. To move in eddies; swirl.

perspective: a particular queen's English, or point in time

fraught: a ledge or rim at the bottom of a cask, or, to have the axes of the eyes not coincident

observatory: parts of which move on hinges, as folding doors, or a fire screen bleat: a crack or aperture through which a liquid might pass

estuary: from where scripture is read

staved: an arch or affected side glance

stove: possessing the property of attracting iron

bouquet: covered with processes or projecting points spreading at right angles or in a greater degree

nape: purpling akin to a bird

threshold: where petals part impetuously

sifting: the ordinary, least recognizable layers of time

describe: promenade vocabulary

plow: antidote to stiffening

circumscribe: walk around a lake

utter: unknown sound of certainty

moan: comfort memorabilia

meander: proceed

contract: to change positions

bewitch: to court favor by low cringing

ampulla: the old name of platinum

amber: a tableland

betide: of the same origin as well, and will

besmear: to welter a swamp

bedaub: to swank or subdue, to wend one's way

muffle: a movement sideways, or an oblique view that may occur when forward speed is unduly diminished

crimson: that portion of a floor of a room on which a fire stands

petal bed: the inner part of anything

alluvial: to happen to befall—come to pass

barricade: to please to such a degree as to smother resistance

the date: a globular bottle, used for holding consecrated oil

holotype: a flask-shaped leaf

footprint: a mirror moved by clockwork, and a fixed object glass, for observing the stars

spiracle: writing in the walls

musk: scent without interruption

ether: being such in name only

bellow: coarse food for livestock

canary: a gownlike outergarment with forelimbs modified to wings

chest: the point directly beneathe the observer

seed: a group of letters representing a word

gosling: to summon return, a speck

suture: to draw or trace a line, to meet or find accidentally

strewn: lowland custard

revel: to form into coils or ringlets

snare: drapery concealing stage from audience

curtsy: an action by one desirous of knowledge

glade: a temporary stillness

doctrine: a small structure on a dome or roof

element: any irresistible influence

wanton: a series of slight rustling sounds

moonwise: a long slender downward curved bill

steep: to mutate muss

ebb: a light saloon

doxology: consisting of bending the knees

sleep: to fasten inaction

thicket: a close-fitting sleeveless jacket of the 16th & 17th centuries

mirror: a person given to jesting

occasion: umbrella-like body, long trailing tentacles

archness: a narrow saw for cutting curves or other difficult lines

blight: black as jet

cowslip: upon the wet moors

eglantine: paramour

timid: of beveled thought

minaret: a slender tower attached to a maiden

sight: cut and polished stone

lowercase: to soften one's words

glass: foam of blossom

entwine: stalk counsellor

book: a folded hour

sail: tongue of woods

loll: invisible thickets

snarl: battle-axe with pointed barbs

lilt: unfretted lute

cloud: attempts to speak aptly

tea: double companion

well: trilling and pipe

star: written in superscript, retinal rising

fox: to dare

gutter: to flag

rain: barefoot, across the courtyard

forest: wallet, axe, cloak, boots

skeleton: hilt and sheathe

sigh: a white garment

glance: a single grace note

page: the barren thicket

skin: answer to abjection

night: cavern

repose: a vague figure in the gleam of the lantern

rumors: goose-pond shipping

cloister: bedclothes

proof: wind, shrilly, in the great ash trees

doze: fairly dark in the parlor

bade: riding out with hawk and hood

haw: little flame

kin: a brooch to take as token

stranger: the lynx was more common

antechamber: wind which darkens the surface of a lake

morning: aperture

mermen: reddish about the feet

dappled: flakes of white birch

ale: pale yellow

freckled: rowan trees thick with berries

tempestuous: forest beastes

dimorphism: woolen brother, silken brother

weatherclouds: for safety's sake, placed farthest from sea

blithe: a lily-rose

trappings: the lappet of a garment or a wing

beacon: to secretly send one a harp

seamarks: white with moss

desist: footprints in snow

diminutive: the blue woman who lives in the glade

monarch: a large sorrel horse

coterie: sheaves of corn

mollify: why the snow wished to lie on the ground

periscope: a room that serves as an entrance to another room

roadsteads: gold with lichen

quaver: far too red and white

purling: a copper horse

vexed: raked with shadows

will: swordfern

farewell: white fields and gray

driven: false tracks

ogress: brow of the wood

vanquished: swallows at the bottom of a lake

cold: a beard falling over the chest

wish: cloth hung from tree

belonging: promontories which keep one from walking

greenwood: distant saber

thyme: optical sachet

maim: to shred flame

howl: coaxed underling

blind: hidden armor

tangled: dubious trawls

tine: dart chamber

unguents: painted eyes of family portraits

headdress: doves which sleep

hunter: hedgehog in bramble

prowl: past the road that led to the house

pincushion: deceived girl

milk teeth: spun sugar

ornament: an owl in a holly tree

supple: a gray mare

to lodge: evening porridge

thistle-seed: falsifiable

keen: plum bun

gravity: a bird's nest

ardent: 'a' was an archer, and shot at the fog

loggia: out of everywhere

locket: handwritten fossil

hansom: forehead smooth and high

lowbrow: from the same box as cherubs' wings

venom: scanty covers

beauty: the science of correct or reliable reasoning

silvering: torch over water

vouchsafed: mirror broken

topside: intertidal mud flats

collapse: secreting or resembling serum

methodology: huntress's nights

piffle: guided by natural law

cuff: vertebrate landfall

benign: alligators' lack

witless: bony fishes

chimera: unlit by star

pillory: winglike pectoral fins

bon mot: a curved wooden club

bonnet: on or near a border

boot black: a rocket used as principal thrust

epaulet: overseas lobule

envoy: a small burrowing

unchaste: an attic

epilogue: a label bearing the owner's name

posy: to induce

lorgnette: shieldlike leaves with narrow openings

forenoon: to open or unlatch

evening: covering of fur

nocturnal: a class of lyric poets from the 12th century

sew: to walk or move with short, affectedly dainty steps

rue: possessive case

ink: ornamental plume

sequester: single plate of glass

katydid: the art of mimicking

plains: a cloth worn by lions

ascension: trow

yoke: sensible walking gown

tenet: the fields are invisible

delve: ebony room

reap: to drown in reverse

russet: brooded wick

pools: sibylline vow

lassitude: sortilege drunk

sumptuous: loggia composed of sails

cleave: granite bounds

bareheaded: enlaced veils

torrent: under rime

becalm: reef-star

scepter: sewer's rubies

amphora: instrumental plumage

aswoon: leonine sob

prow: giddy horses

lightning: filigree reeds

guardian: vaporous flowers

carbon: sister-of-pearl

ash: daughter-of-wood

chaste: cordials and clocks

gnaw: ravenous grot

limpid: pouring potions

kohl: cups of snow

haggard: hissing ruins

fling: votive tincture

attar: jewelbox weeps

succor: slate lozenge

iris: filament knotted

presence: swollen ether

pedestal: husk omen

The Traveling Crystal

Chrystallum, or clear ice, viewed merely as another state

xi.

Emblem scrawl
Facet hand
Slant door
Hood wound
Haze goblet
Cut provocation
Light injection
Askew element

Lullaby

O the windward—it is a sooth
that harbors through the withering

O the saith it is a dormer
that bids the sooth to enter

and let us sake the seer my fro
and let us sister together

the singer lasts the secant long
somnambulism lasts formally

and let us saint the seam my frieze
and let us sip together

the singer lasts the secret long
but this somewhere lasts foretellingly